ISBN 9798543054550

Research and interior design by Ryan Haag.

Cover and graphic design by Shalone Cason, www.sdcason.com

This book is best viewed and colored on its side.

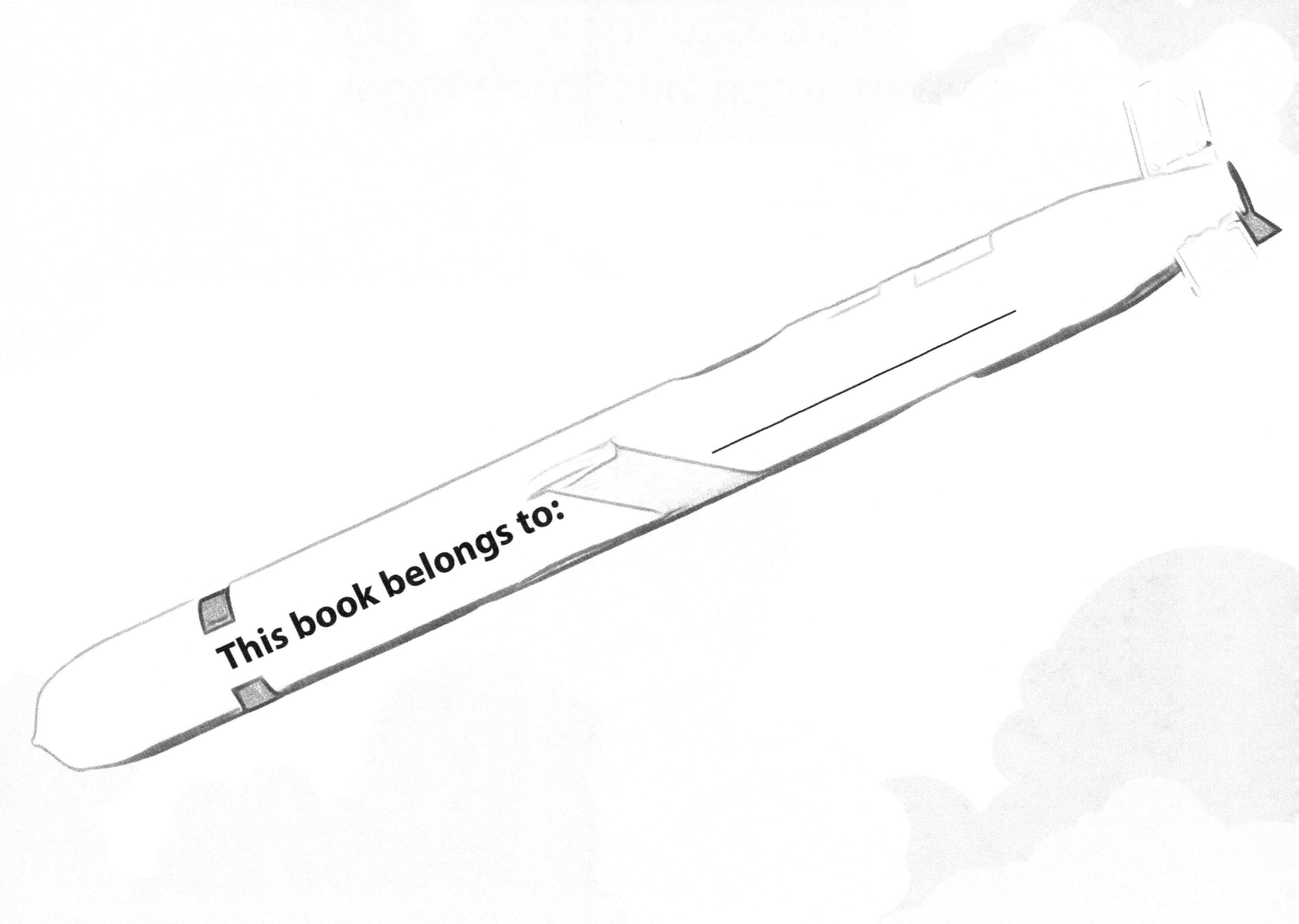
This book belongs to:

The amphibious transport dock ship USS Green Bay fires a Rolling Airframe Missile. The RIM-116 missile actually rolls in flight to allow it to better see electromagnetic waves.

The guided missile destroyer USS John Paul Jones launches a Standard Missile-6 (SM-6) in 2014. The SM-6 the SM-6 can fly over 3 times the speed of sound and can reach targets over 100 miles away.

The U.S. Navy the guided missile destroyer USS King (DDG-41) with the RIM-67A surface-to-air training missiles. The RIM-67A has been retired and is now used as a supersonic test target.

This is an vehicle equipped with a Naval Strike Missile. Used by the Marine Corps and called NMESIS, this allows the Marines to engage and destroy ships from a beach landing site.

R02G

A Long Range Anti-Ship Missile (LRASM) fired from an F/A-18 in 2019. The LRASM is the Navy's next generation of long-range, air-launched anti-ship missiles.

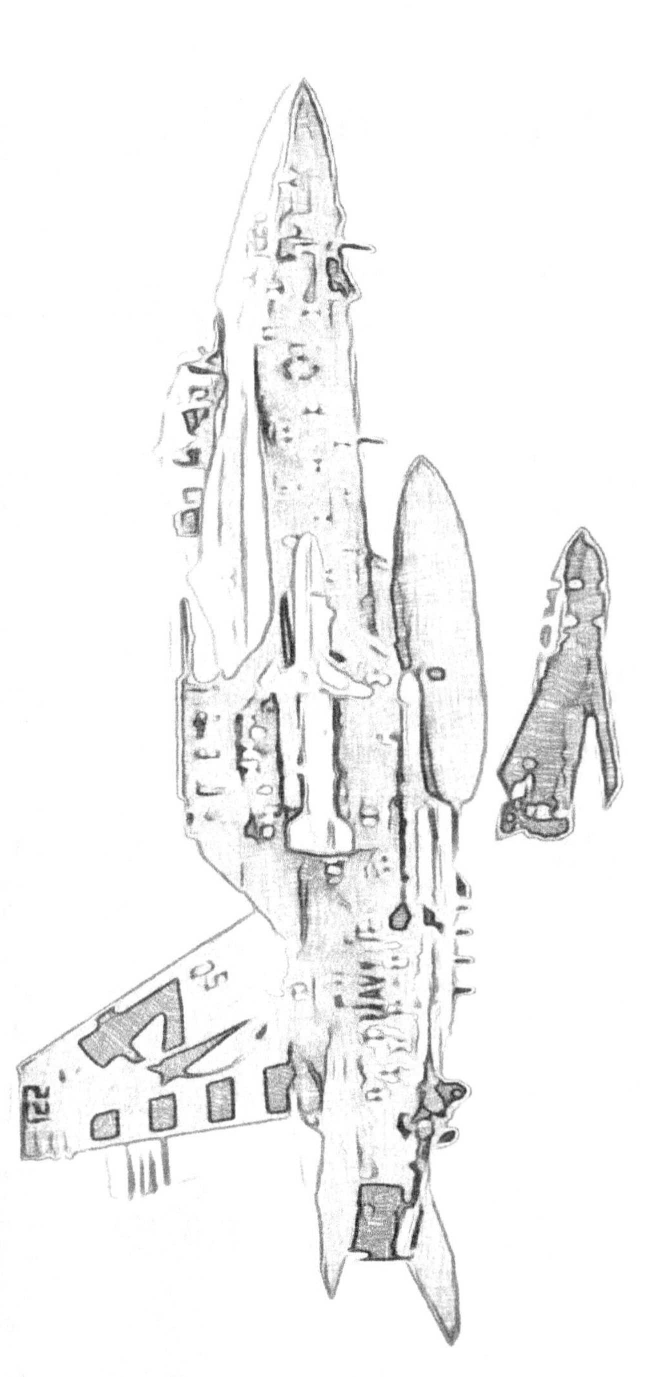

An F/A-18C Hornet armed with ten AIM-120B missiles and two AIM-9L Sidewinder missiles, one on each wing tip. These missiles are all designed to destroy other aircraft.

16
16

A Raytheon SM-2 Block IIIA guided missile explodes over USS The Sullivans during a training exercise on July 18, 2015. Thankfully, nobody was injured in the explosion.

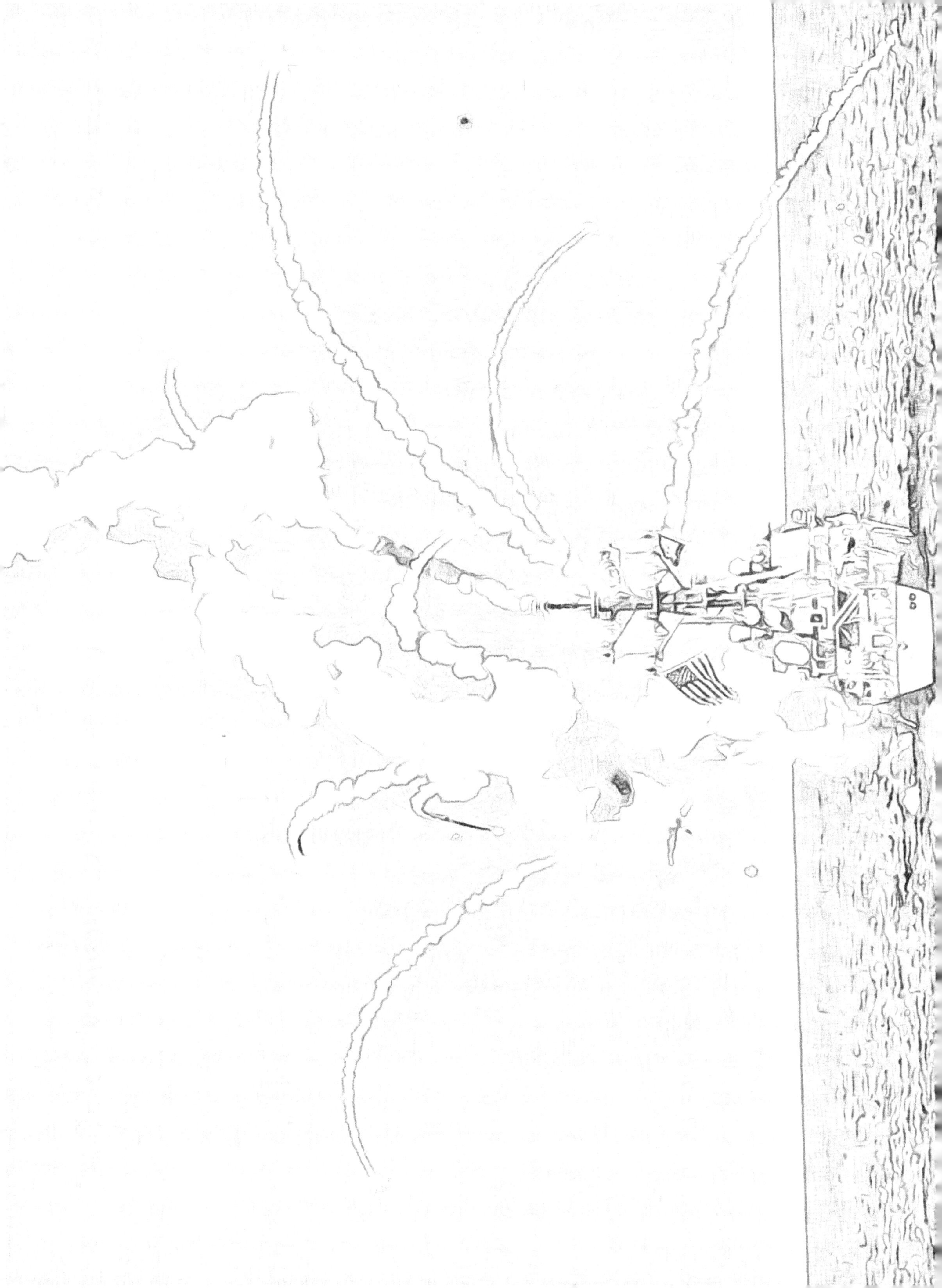

Flight crews load an inert Captive Air Training Missile (CATM-9) on a F/A-18F Super Hornet. Training missiles allow aviators to safely practice operating with missiles during training missions.

A Tomahawk Land Attack Missile (TLAM) striking a training target, just before impact. The TLAM is a subsonic cruise missile launched from surface ships and submarines that is designed to attack land targets almost 1,000 miles away.

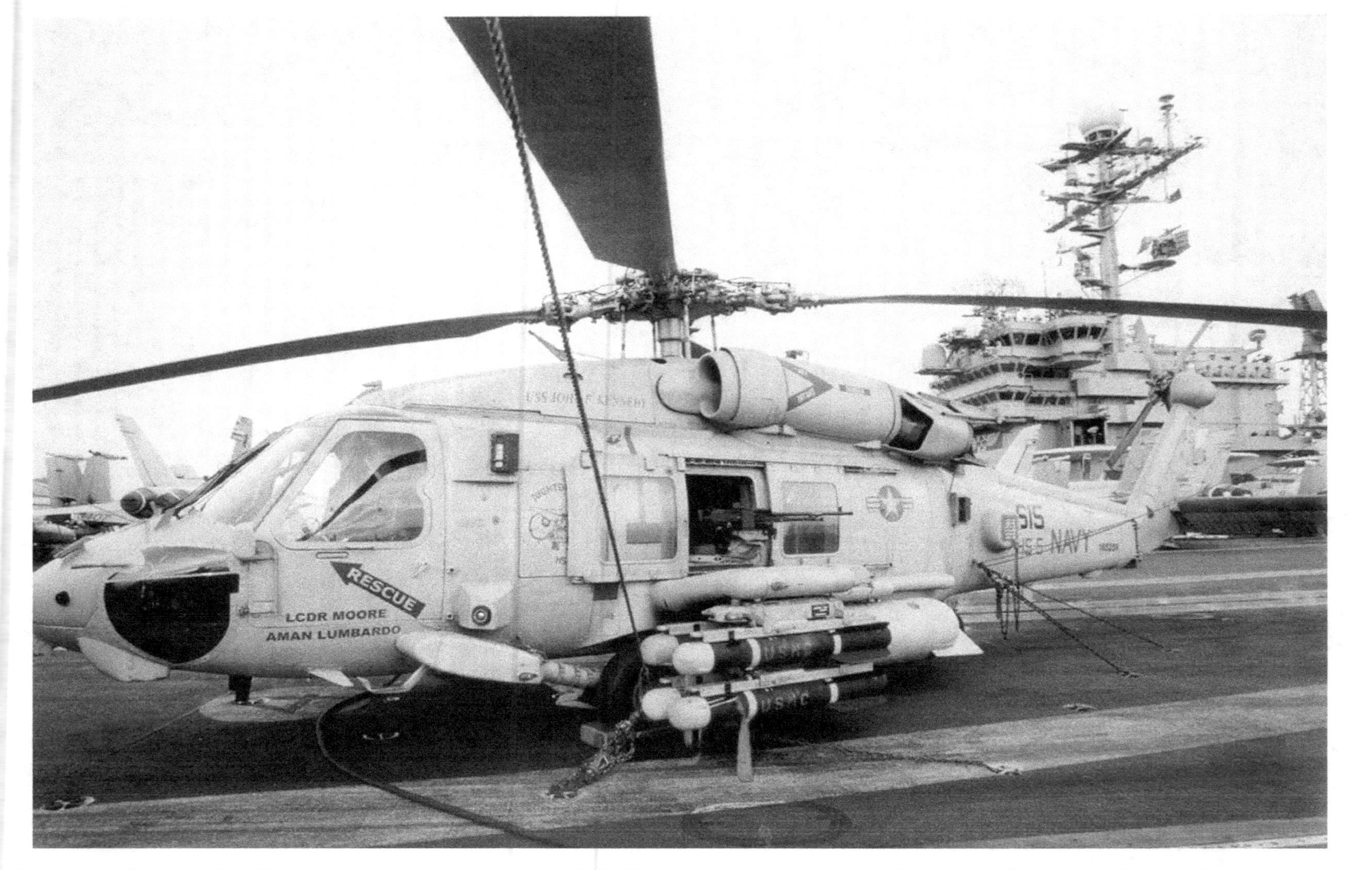

Multiple AGM-114 Hellfire missiles loaded onto a Navy helicopter. The Hellfire is a laser guided, fire-and-forget missile designed to attack land and sea targets from an aircraft.

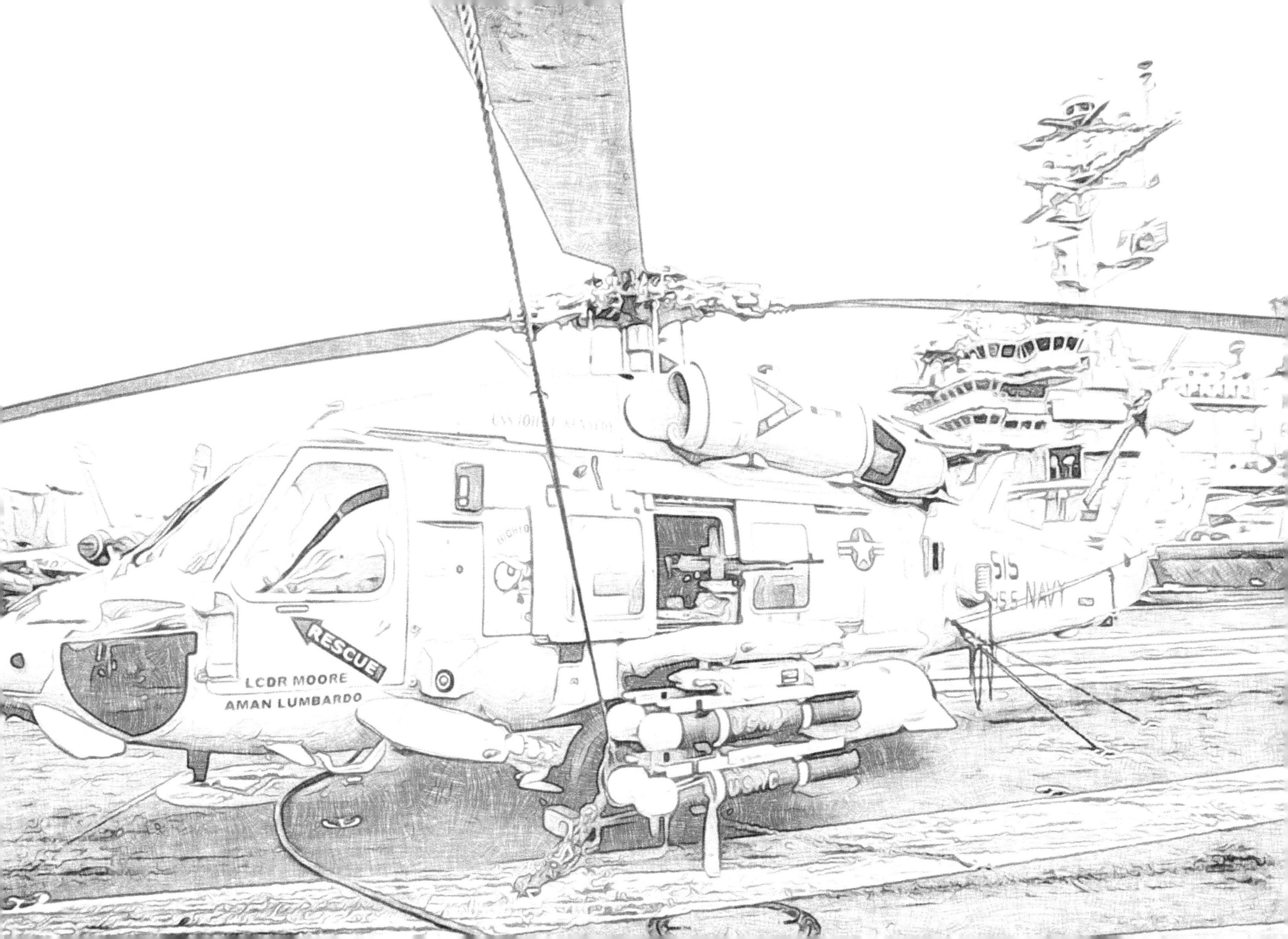

NAVY
515
RESCUE
LCDR MOORE
AMAN LUMBARDO

An evolved sea sparrow missile (ESSM) launches from one of USS Gerald R. Ford's (CVN 78) weapons sponsons during combat systems ship qualification trials. The ESSM is an upgraded missile, designed to intercept supersonic missiles and aircraft.

The littoral combat ship USS Gabrielle Giffords (LCS 10) launches a Naval Strike Missile. The Naval Strike Missile is a long-range, precision strike weapon that destroys enemy ships.

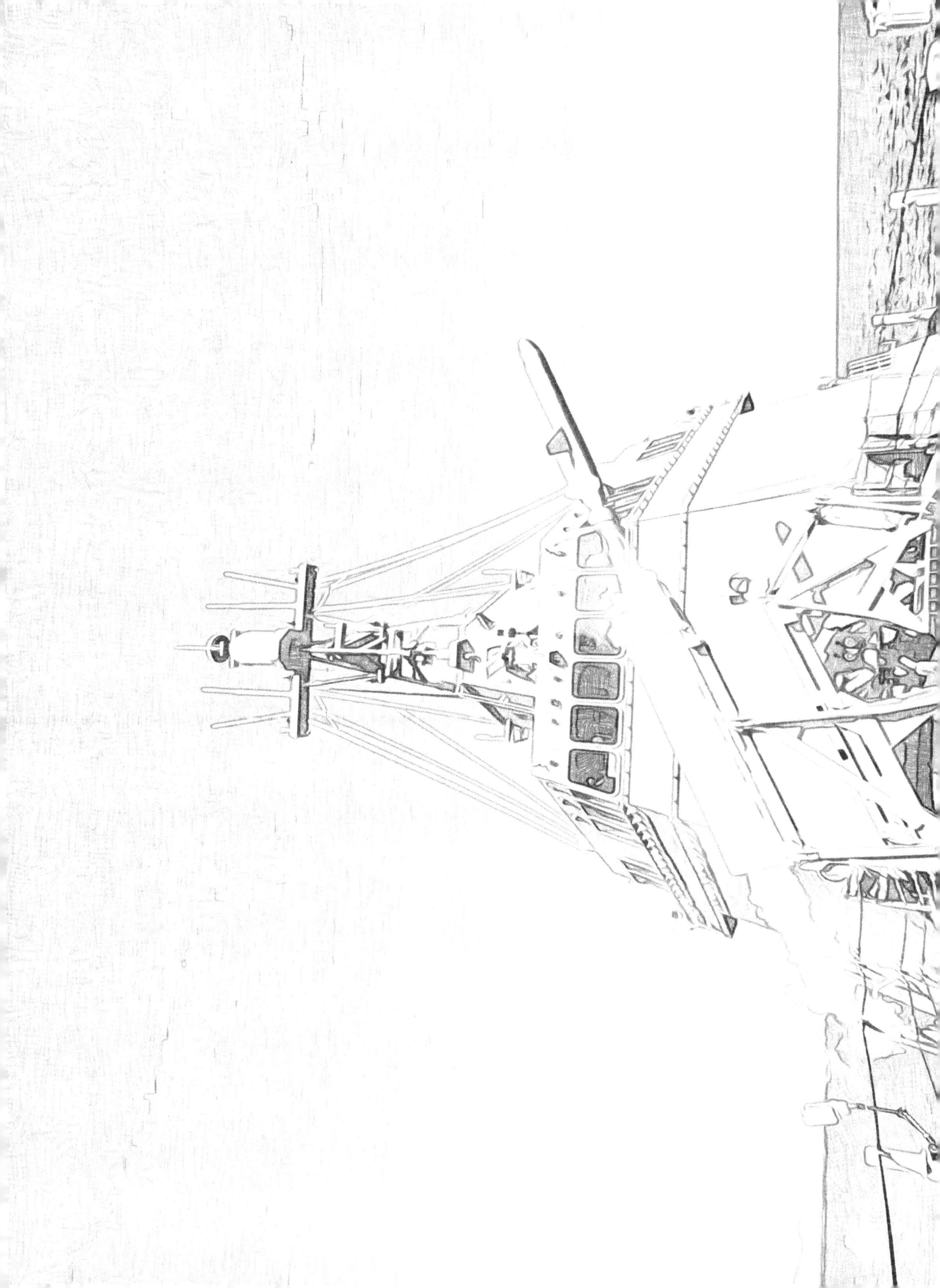

The Arleigh Burke-class guided-missile destroyer USS John S. McCain (DDG 56) launches a Standard Missile (SM) 2 during a missile exercise. The SM-2 is designed to destroy incoming anti-ship missiles and aircraft.

An F-35C Lightning II (Joint Strike Fighter) fires a AIM-120 missile. The AIM-120 is an air-to-air missile designed to shoot down other aircraft.

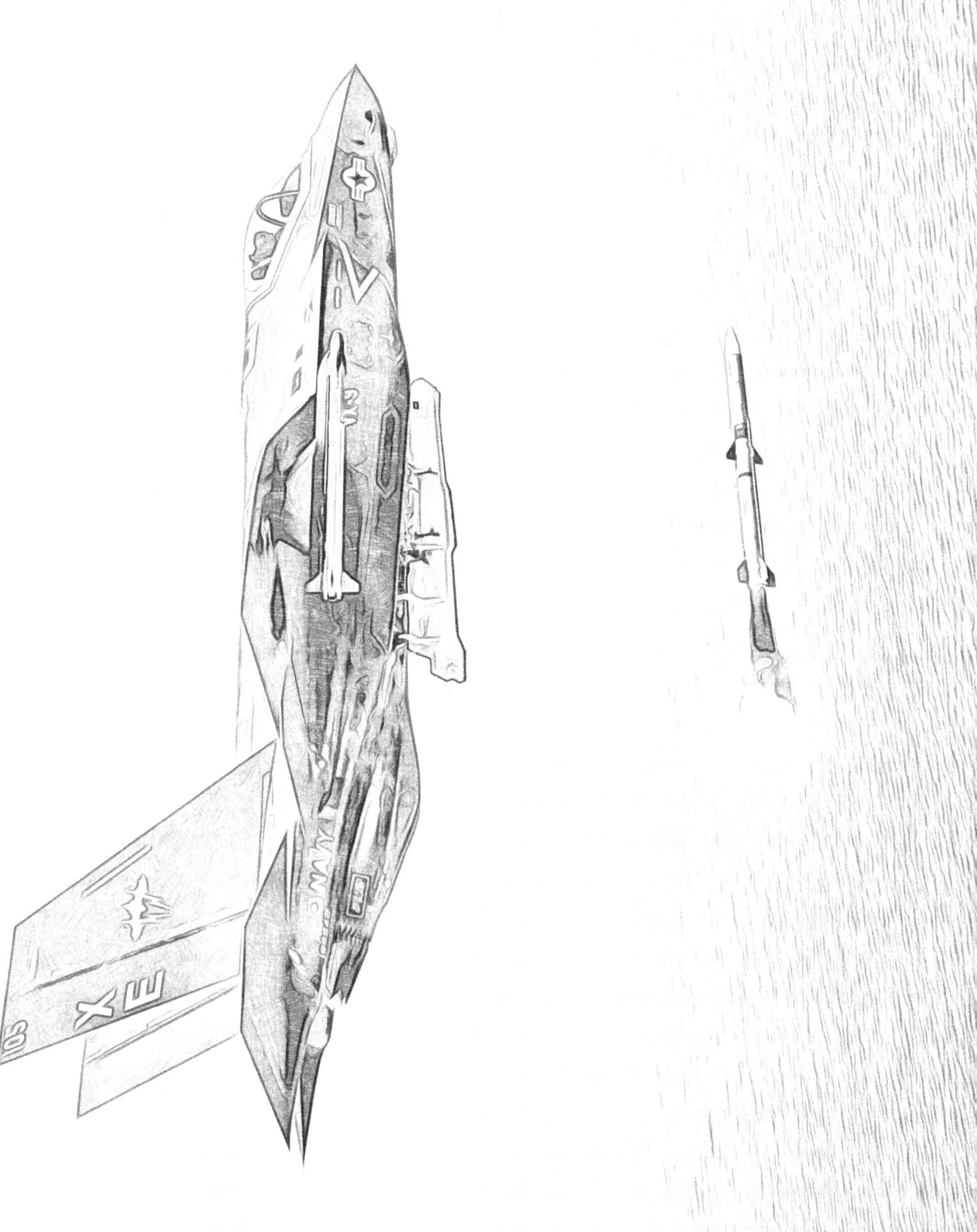

The Ticonderoga-class cruiser USS Chancellorsville (CG 62) launched a Standard Missile (SM) 2 in the Philippine Sea. The SM-2 is designed to destroy incoming missiles and aircraft over 90 miles away.

The amphibious dock landing ship USS Ashland (LSD 48) launches a Rolling Airframe Missile (RAM) in the Pacific Ocean. The RAM is designed to protect a ship from incoming missiles.

The Ticonderoga-class cruiser USS Chancellorsville (CG 62) fires a Harpoon Missile. The Harpoon is a subsonic, sea-skimming anti-ship missile used by over 30 countries around the world.

The guided missile destroyer USS John Paul Jones launches a Standard Missile-6 in 2014.

A Regulus missile test launch aboard the USS Randolph (CV-15). The Regulus missile was the first nuclear missile launched from both surface ships and submarines. It flew 500 miles and was used in the Navy from 1955 until 1964.

A Griffin missile is launched from coastal patrol ship USS Thunderbolt (PC 12) during a MK-60 Griffin guided missile system shoot. The Griffin is a small, light weight, low-cost missile designed to intercept fast moving small boats.

An unarmed Trident II D5 missile launches from the Ohio-class ballistic missile submarine USS Nebraska (SSBN 739). The Trident II D5 is a nuclear submarine-launched missile that is integral to the defense of the United States.

An AGM-65 Maverick training missile is loaded onto a P-3C Orion maritime patrol aircraft at Naval Air Station Sigonella. The AGM-65 is an air-to-ground missile that can destroy a wide range of targets from over 12 miles away.

COMMANDING OFFICER
CDR GONZALO PARTIDA
406
WARNING

The guided-missile destroyer USS Fitzgerald
(DDG 62) launches a Standard Missile-3 (SM-3).
The RIM-161 SM-3 is designed to intercept
ballistic missiles over 500 miles away.

An F/A-18F Super Hornet with an AGM-88E Advanced Anti-Radiation Guided Missile. The AGM-88E is designed to attack radar antennas, can fly at twice the speed of sound and travel over 90 miles.

121
STRIKE TEST
121
SD
VX-23
NAVY
166449

If you enjoyed this coloring book, please be sure to leave us a quick online review on Amazon! Every five star review helps more people find and enjoy these coloring books!